The Seven Gifts of the Holy Spirit

Most Rev. Arthur J. Serratelli
S.T.D., S.S.L., D.D.

CATHOLIC BOOK PUBLISHING CORP.
New Jersey

NIHIL OBSTAT: Rev. T. Kevin Corcoran, MA
Censor Librorum

IMPRIMATUR: ✠ Most Rev. David M. O'Connell, C.M., J.C.D., D.D.
Bishop of Trenton

June 25, 2018

Acts—Acts of the Apostles	Jdt—Judith	Phil—Philippians
Am—Amos	Jer—Jeremiah	Phlm—Philemon
Bar—Baruch	Jgs—Judges	Prv—Proverbs
1 Chr—1 Chronicles	Jl—Joel	Ps(s)—Psalms
2 Chr—2 Chronicles	Jn—John	1 Pt—1 Peter
Col—Colossians	1 Jn—1 John	2 Pt—2 Peter
1 Cor—1 Corinthians	2 Jn—2 John	Rom—Romans
2 Cor—2 Corinthians	3 Jn—3 John	Ru—Ruth
Dn—Daniel	Jon—Jonah	Rv—Revelation
Dt—Deuteronomy	Jos—Joshua	Sir—Sirach
Eccl—Ecclesiastes	Jude—Jude	1 Sm—1 Samuel
Eph—Ephesians	1 Kgs—1 Kings	2 Sm—2 Samuel
Est—Esther	2 Kgs—2 Kings	Song—Song of Songs
Ex—Exodus	Lam—Lamentations	Tb—Tobit
Ez—Ezekiel	Lk—Luke	1 Thes—1 Thessalonians
Ezr—Ezra	Lv—Leviticus	2 Thes—2 Thessalonians
Gal—Galatians	Mal—Malachi	Ti—Titus
Gn—Genesis	1 Mc—1 Maccabees	1 Tm—1 Timothy
Hb—Habakkuk	2 Mc—2 Maccabees	2 Tm—2 Timothy
Heb—Hebrews	Mi—Micah	Wis—Wisdom
Hg—Haggai	Mk—Mark	Zec—Zechariah
Hos—Hosea	Mt—Matthew	Zep—Zephaniah
Is—Isaiah	Na—Nahum	
Jas—James	Neh—Nehemiah	
Jb—Job	Nm—Numbers	
	Ob—Obadiah	

(T-930)

ISBN 978-1-947070-23-3

© 2018 Catholic Book Publishing Corp., N.J.

Printed in Canada

www.catholicbookpublishing.com

Contents

Introduction

Benjamin Franklin holds the great distinction of being not only one of America's founding fathers, but also one of her most cherished sons. He was a statesman, writer, inventor, and philosopher. In our age of increasing specialization, the breadth of his contributions staggers the mind. The Franklin stove, the lightning rod, swim fins, the glass armonica, the flexible catheter, and bifocal eyeglasses, to name a few.

Franklin has also left behind a rich literary legacy. He wrote essays, books, and newspaper articles. He penned letters and composed ballads. He wrote an illustrious autobiography. But, he is best known for *Poor Richard's Almanac*.

In 1732, Franklin published it for the first time. The pamphlet contained a calendar, seasonal weather forecasts, practical household hints, puzzles, poems, and astronomical information. *Poor Richard's Almanac* quickly became a bestseller in the American colonies. No doubt the many witty aphorisms sprinkled throughout the pamphlet made it so popular.

In many ways, *Poor Richard's Almanac* is a repository of the wit and wisdom of Franklin himself. In fact, many of his wise sayings have become proverbial. *"Well done is better than well said." "An investment in knowledge pays the best interest." "It is the working man who is the happy man. It is the idle man who is the miserable man." "Early to bed and early to rise makes a man healthy, wealthy, and wise." "God helps them that help themselves."*

Franklin's wisdom sayings help us in our own search for living a good life. They are expressions of good common sense. They remain timely, because *"common sense is not so common"* (Voltaire). Franklin understood the holistic connection between mind, body, and spirit. His bits of advice aim to help others make that connection and have a happy life. In this regard, his sayings are close cousins to the Wisdom Literature of the Old Testament.

Biblical wisdom (*hokmah*) includes both a practical and a speculative aspect. At times, it resembles in tone and purpose the advice of a Franklin, an Epicurus, or a Marcus Aurelius. It passes on the accumulated knowledge of many generations on how to make the best of daily situations. At other times, biblical wisdom soars high above prosaic aphorisms to the poetic heights of lofty meditation on the very purpose of life and human suffering.

In the Old Testament, the wise person is the one who knows how to ply his craft (see Ex 35:25-26), the one who can make right judgments (see 1 Kgs 3:1-15); and, the one whose moral behavior is upright (see Prv 24:29). Wisdom gradually comes to be identified with the law (see Sir 24:23-24) that provides God's plan for our happiness. And, ultimately, it is personified to the point of identifying it with God Himself (see Prv 8:1-31; Wis 6:12-21).

The New Testament sees wisdom as the plan *"mysterious, hidden, which God predetermined before the ages for our glory"* (1 Cor 2:7). And, the New Testament identifies Jesus Himself as the very Wisdom of God (see 1 Cor 1:24; Col 1:15-18). *"In Him has been revealed in a new and more wonderful way the fundamental truth concerning creation"* (Pope St. John Paul II, *Redemptor hominis*, 8). He is the *"New Adam [who]...*

fully reveals man to himself..." (Gaudium et Spes, 22).

Isaiah prophesied the coming of Jesus as the long-awaited Messiah who, as Wisdom Incarnate, leads us to God. This prophet living eight centuries before Christ said of Him, *"The spirit of the Lord shall rest upon him: a spirit of wisdom and of understanding, a spirit of counsel and of strength, a spirit of knowledge and of fear of the Lord"* (Is 11: 2). It is from these words of Isaiah that the Church speaks of the seven gifts of the Holy Spirit. They are wisdom, understanding, counsel, fortitude, knowledge, piety, and fear of the Lord.

The Hebrew text of Isaiah lists seven gifts, but it actually mentions the fear of the Lord twice. However, the Greek Septuagint and Latin Vulgate list seven different gifts, mentioning "fear of the Lord" only once and including "piety." Since the early Church adopted the Greek Septuagint and the Latin Vulgate, the Church has traditionally taught that there are seven gifts of the Holy Spirit. Seven is the number of perfection. And, the Holy Spirit generously bestows these gifts on believers.

Jesus alone possessed the seven gifts of the Holy Spirit in their fullness. But, the Holy Spirit graciously gives those same gifts to all who follow Jesus. In Baptism, we are clothed with Christ and become a member of His Body the Church, sharing in His dignity as priest, prophet, and king. In Confirmation, we are sealed with the Holy Spirit so that, through His holy anointing, we *"may be conformed more perfectly to Christ, the Son of God"* (*The Rite of Confirmation*). As St. Paul teaches, *"For those whom he foreknew he also predestined to be conformed to the image of his Son ..."* (Rom 8:29). Through the grace of Baptism and Confirmation, we take on the identity of Christ. We become one with Him and come to share those seven gifts given to Him as Messiah. Blessed with the seven gifts of the Holy Spirit, we continue His work in our world.

The seven gifts are our inheritance as baptized and confirmed Christians. We do not earn them. We do not merit them. They are given to us gratuitously. They make us open to the promptings of the Holy Spirit in our lives. They help us grow in holiness, making us fit for heaven.

These seven gifts of the Holy Spirit help us live a truly authentic Christian way of life. As the *Catechism of the Catholic Church* teaches, *"The moral life of Christians is sustained by the gifts of the Holy Spirit. These are permanent dispositions which make a person docile in following the promptings of the Holy Spirit. . . .They complete and perfect the virtues of those who receive them. . . readily obeying divine inspirations"* (Catechism of the Catholic Church, **1830-31**).

CHAPTER 1

The Gift of Wisdom
Living in Friendship with God

With its white marble glistening in the hot sun, the ruins of Athens' acropolis towers high over the city below. From ancient times, the Parthenon has crowned the acropolis. It was the greatest sanctuary of the most important city of classical Greece. This magnificent temple housed the forty foot statue of Athena, the virgin goddess of reason and the city's patroness. Art historians consider this statue of Athena as one of the greatest achievements of sculpture. Covered with more than 1,500 pounds of solid gold, this statue was the single greatest financial asset of ancient Athens. However, the Parthenon was much more than the repository of this precious cult image.

The Parthenon was a living monument to the values and ideals of ancient Greece. The Greeks strove for *symmetria*, i.e., the balance and harmony of part to part and each part to the whole. They strove for perfection. And the Parthenon, with its faultless proportion, precision, and balance was the apotheosis of this striving. By honoring Athena, the female god of wisdom, within such a perfectly constructed temple, the Greeks acknowledged that they needed wisdom to achieve the perfection that they sought not only in art, but in life as well.

It belongs to the human spirit to strive for perfection. We are always searching for something greater, for more knowledge, more practical and theoretical know-how in order to improve our human condition. But, we need not just knowledge. We require wisdom. They are not identical. It is one thing to know *how* to do something. It takes wisdom to know *when* to do it. Wisdom guides us in the use of our knowledge. Two individuals may know how to wield a knife. A fool uses it to inflict harm and even death on someone. A surgeon wisely uses it to bring healing and life to another.

Many discoveries in medicine and science have given us great knowledge that has transformed our lives. We know so much more than our grandparents about the miracle of conception and birth. But, some people use that knowledge foolishly to destroy God's precious gift of life. We have a greater knowledge of the physical universe and know how to harness the power of the atom. Wisdom insures that we use that power for energy and growth and not for destruction and death. We desperately need wisdom.

King Solomon is the most famous biblical example of wisdom. At the age of twelve, when he was about to be anointed as king, he prayed not for wealth, fame, or success. He asked God neither for a long life nor happiness. No! He asked for wisdom. God answered him, saying, *"I do as you requested. I give you a heart so wise and discerning that there has never been anyone like you until now, nor after you will there be anyone to equal you"* (1 Kgs 3:12).

Wisdom was not something Solomon acquired. It was not merely natural intelligence. It was something more. It was a gift from God who gave him the ability to see beyond circumstances to the truth. That is why, immediately following God's bestowal of the gift of wisdom, the Scriptures record Solomon's famous judgment given to two prostitutes.

Both women had given birth. One child died. Both women came to Solomon, each claiming that the child who lived was hers. Solomon knew the heart of a true mother.

So he announced that the child should be cut in half and each woman given half. One woman accepted his decision. The other woman cried out not to harm the baby. He returned the live child to the second woman, the baby's true mother (see 1 Kgs 3:16-28). He realized that a mother always desires life for the child of her womb. He was, indeed, the wisest of all.

Daniel is another biblical figure of great wisdom. The prophet Ezekiel mentions Daniel along with Noah and Job as righteous individuals who, by their wisdom, saved others (see Ez 14:14). Daniel was a young man taken into exile from Judah by the Babylonians in the sixth century before Christ. Like Joseph who, by his wisdom, rose to great influence in the court of Pharaoh, Daniel became an important advisor to the Babylonian and Persian kings because of his wisdom.

In the second century before Christ, Antiochus IV Epiphanes, the Seleucid successor to half of Alexander the Great's kingdom, was using Hellenization as the weapon to establish his totalitarian rule over his territories. In Judea and Samaria, he was persecuting observant Jews who practiced the rite of circumcision, studied the Torah, and kept their dietary laws.

Antiochus IV Epiphanes even went as far as placing a statue of Zeus in the Temple in Jerusalem, ordering the Jews to worship it (see 2 Mac 6:1–12). This sacrilegious outrage sparked the revolt of the Maccabees lasting from 167 to 160 B.C. During this period of intense persecution, the Jews sought solace in the stories that they had heard about Daniel. They collected these accounts and put them into the Book of Daniel. Daniel was a true model for them to follow in a time when their faith was being sorely tested.

When the Babylonians destroyed Jerusalem, Nebuchadnezzar, king of Babylon, took the young Daniel and his friends Hananiah, Mishael, and Azariah as captives back to Babylon. He gave them new names (Shadrach, Meshach, and Abednego), educated them in the ways of his own nation, and attached them to court, providing them with an abundance of luxuries. All with the purpose of using them as his instruments to control his Jewish subjects in exile.

The four young men served the king loyally, while never becoming disloyal to their faith. They refused to eat the rich fare of meat that the king sent them, because it had been sacrificed to idols. Their refusal exemplifies the great truth that religion concerns even the details of our daily life. Dedication to God in the smallest things is not scrupulousness, but the greatest loyalty. Because they would not allow themselves to be defiled by their pagan surroundings, God blessed them and *"gave knowledge and... wisdom... "* (Dn 1:17). Their wisdom was *"ten times better"* than any of the wise men at the king's court.

When Nebuchadnezzar had a most disturbing dream, not one of his wise men could reveal its meaning. On learning that the king had ordered all of his wise men to be executed for their failure to interpret his dream, Daniel entreated his friends to join with him in prayer to God. Friends who pray for one another and with one another are always a great blessing to each other. Their prayers of intercession call down on each the mercy of God. In answer to the prayers of Daniel and his friends, God revealed the secret of the king's dream to Daniel in a vision.

Prayer should always accompany all we do. Like Daniel who prayed before he stood before the king to interpret his dream, we should not undertake any good work before going to God in prayer. And, like Daniel who immediately burst into grateful praise of God who *"gives wisdom to the wise and knowledge to those who understand"* (Dn 2:21), we should always return in thanksgiving to God for His gifts. For wisdom is always a gift from God.

So important was the gift of wisdom given to Daniel that a second century Hellenistic Jew, translating the Hebrew Bible into Greek, rearranged the chapters of his translation of the book of Daniel. In his version called the *Theodotion*, the translator placed the story of Susanna, found in chapter thirteen in all other versions, as an introduction to the book. He wanted his readers to realize that all the stories of Daniel in the book exemplify the wisdom which Daniel displays so admirably in the story of Susanna.

In the story, Susanna is a very attractive married woman. As she bathes modestly in her garden, she becomes the unwitting victim of two lecherous elders. Hidden in the garden, they wait until her attendants have left. Then they try to force her to have relations with them. They threaten her, trying to coerce her into submission. If she refuses, they warn her, they will accuse her of having a secret encounter with a young male lover.

Susanna must choose. If she yields to their lustful desires, she disobeys the Law of Moses. If she resists, she faces the accusations of the two elders. Since her word would mean nothing against the testimony of two respected elders, she can only expect the inevitable penalty of death for adultery (see Lev 20:10; Dt 22:22). Nonetheless, Susanna resists. She will not be forced to sin. She willingly accepts the consequences of her fidelity to God and to her husband.

Just as the proceedings against her come to a grim conclusion and she is about to be dragged off to her death, *"God [stirs] up the holy spirit of a young boy named Daniel... and he [cries] aloud: 'I am innocent of this woman's blood'"* (Dn 13:45-46). Moved by the Spirit, Daniel is confident that he can save Susanna from an unjust death. After separating the two elders, he cross examines them about the location of the lovers' intimacies. The first elder says that he saw Susanna and her lover under a mastic tree. The second, under an oak. The mastic grows to thirteen feet high; the oak, fifty feet high. Their own words prove their guilt. Susanna is saved and the elders condemned.

Those who read this story in the Greek text would have delighted in the turn of fate based on a turn of phrases. When the first elder says that he saw Susanna under the mastic tree (σχίνον: *skinon*), Daniel responds by saying that an angel is ready to cut him in two (σχίσει: *schisei*). When the second elder names the oak tree (πρίνον: *prinon*), Daniel says that an angel is ready to saw him in two (πρίσαι: *prisai*). Ironically, the trees that the elders name provide the raw material for Daniel's clever play on words that turns their accusation against Susanna into their own death sentence.

In this brief, vivid narrative of Susanna as well as in the account of Nebuchadnezzar's dream, Daniel emerges a paradigm of wisdom. His is a wisdom that does not come from human effort. Neither careful observation of the world nor serious academic study provided Daniel with wisdom. God did! Because Daniel stood apart from the pagan culture that surrounded him and stood open before God in prayer, God gifted him with such great wisdom.

For each of us, Daniel stands forth as a model of how to live in a culture that rejects and mocks Christian values. It is not the environment that makes the person. It is each of us who shape our environment. To those who remain loyal to the faith and who pray, God is eager to grant the wisdom to dispel ignorance, to make right decisions, and to triumph over any adversity. In fact, He has already given us the wisdom to transform the world.

Wisdom is one of the gifts of the Holy Spirit (see Is 11:2). It equips us to deal with the practical details of life in light of God's ultimate purpose for His creation. The gift of wisdom enables us to judge the things of this world as God sees them. *"It is simply this: Seeing the world situations, conjunctures, problems, everything with God's eyes. . . Often we see things as we want to see them or according to our heart, with love, with hate, with envy. Wisdom is what the Holy Spirit does within us so that we can see everything with God's eyes. This is the gift of wisdom"* (Pope Francis, General Audience, April 9, 2014).

By the gift of wisdom, we see beyond the particulars of success and failure, trials and triumphs, joys and sorrows of everyday life to the plan of God Who orders all according to His will for our good. Our minds are lifted above the mundane to contemplate divine truths. No matter what the level of our formal education in the faith, with the gift of wisdom we can reach a profound knowledge of the divine.

Enlightened by the gift of wisdom, we judge rightly between morally good acts that lead us to God and evil acts that distance us from Him. We recognize ourselves and others as called to the supernatural dignity of becoming sons and daughters of God. We see others and love others more and more as God sees and loves them. We direct our human thoughts, feelings, words, and deeds according to the ultimate destiny that God has for all of us. We are not held captive to the ideology of a particular age, but truly enjoy the freedom of the children of God.

Wisdom is not just one of the gifts of the Holy Spirit. It is the first gift that Isaiah the prophet lists as given to the Messiah (see Is 11:2). It has the place of primacy among the gifts of the Holy Spirit because it is essential for living life as it was meant to be lived in friendship with God and in harmony with all creation, even as Jesus himself lived. In our increasingly secular age, wisdom is a gift most desperately needed!

CHAPTER 2

The Gift of Understanding
Seeing through the Heart

All of science is born of observing and understanding. When a scientist is keen in observing even everyday experiences, new discoveries come about. For example, on September 3, 1928, Scottish biologist Alexander Fleming returned from a much needed vacation from his work. After his August break, he went into his laboratory where he had been experimenting with bacteria in petri dishes. He observed that, while he was away, a strange mold had grown on the dishes and had killed off the surrounding bacteria. A light went off in his mind and modern medicine has never been the same. He understood what had happened. And, his understanding led him to the discovery of penicillin that has saved countless lives.

Over 2,000 years earlier, a similar moment of understanding flashed across the mind of Archimedes. He was the greatest mathematician of antiquity and one of the greatest of physicists, engineers, inventors, and astronomers of all time. Hieron II, the King of Syracuse in Sicily, had ordered a crown to be made of gold. However, he wanted to be sure that the goldsmith did not substitute some silver for some of the gold in order to make himself a greater profit. He asked Archimedes to solve the problem without destroying the crown.

Archimedes spent hours trying to find a way to determine whether or not the crown was pure gold. He already knew that gold was denser than silver and that a gold crown would occupy less space than a crown made of gold and silver. Then, one day, as he was stepping into his bathtub, he noticed more and more water was displaced. Observing what was happening, he immediately understood the principle of buoyancy and how it could be used to determine the amount of gold in the crown. So excited by his discovery, he immediately jumped out of his bath and, so the legend says, ran through the streets crying, *"Eureka!"* ("I found the answer!").

As in the case of Archimedes in his bathtub and Fleming in his laboratory, our knowledge and understanding starts from the outside with our five senses. We interact with the things around us. We observe the world around us, think about it, and try to understand it. As St. Thomas Aquinas writes, *"Now it is natural to man to attain to intellectual truths through sensible objects, because all of our knowledge originates from the senses"* (*Summa Theologica*, 1, a.1. 9c). We are matter and spirit, senses and intellect. We begin with the material, but we can arrive through our intellect at the spiritual, the transcendental, and the immaterial.

Since our intellect is limited, the Holy Spirit gives us the gift of understanding to help us comprehend the truths of our faith. This gift enables us to go beyond the boundaries of human reason and attain a knowledge that we could not reach on our own.

By faith, we give intellectual assent to truths that are divinely revealed, such as the divinity of Christ and the mystery of the Eucharist. We believe these truths because we accept the authority of God Who reveals them. By the gift of understanding, we penetrate into the meaning of these truths. The gift of understanding, infused by the Holy Spirit, gives us a way to grasp easily and deeply the truths given us by God and to comprehend how truths known by reason are related to our supernatural destiny. It assists us in seeing how God's eternal truths serve as standards for human conduct and help us do the good deeds that we ought to do.

By the gift of understanding, we come to penetrate more deeply into the words of Sacred Scripture. We see beyond the surface meaning of the text to its relation to Jesus, the Word Incarnate. We come to understand how, in the events of the Old Testament, the mystery of our redemption in Christ is already prefigured. As St. Augustine taught, *"The New Testament is hidden in the Old; the Old is made accessible by the New."*

For example, at the command of his father Abraham, Isaac carried the wood for a sacrifice to the top of Mt. Moriah. Isaac saw only the fire and wood for the sacrifice and innocently asked his father where the lamb for sacrifice was (see Gn 22:7). Abraham answered, *"God will provide himself the lamb ..."* (Gn 22:8). The Father did provide the lamb by sending His son as our redeemer. Already in this event, Jesus is prefigured. For, in obedience to the Father's will, Jesus carries the wood of the Cross up the hill of Golgotha for the perfect sacrifice that redeems the world.

Enlightened by the Holy Spirit, we understand the deeper meaning of John the Baptist's words to his own disciples when he points Jesus out to them, saying *"Behold, the Lamb of God, who takes away the sin of the world!"* (Jn 1:29). During His public ministry, people call him "Messiah," "Rabbi," "Son of God", "Savior" and "Lord." But, "the Lamb of God" is the first title given to Jesus by anyone in all four gospels.

The Baptist gives this title to Jesus at the time of the Passover. The highways are crowded with people bringing their one-year-old lambs to be sacrificed in the Temple in Jerusalem. In full view of these lambs, John the Baptist calls Jesus "the Lamb of God" because from the very beginning of His life, Jesus has come to sacrifice Himself for our sins.

What the many sacrifices of the former covenant promised, Jesus fulfills. He is the Lamb not provided by man, but by God Himself. God, who spared Isaac, *"did not spare his own Son but handed him over for us"* (Rom 8:32). With the gift of understanding, therefore, we recognize Jesus as the Beloved Son Who offers His life in the one true sacrifice that brings God's blessing on all people, as He had sworn to Abraham.

By the gift of understanding, we also come to see beneath events of our lives the overarching providence of God. We recognize the hand of God not only in the joys we experience, but also in the trials and sufferings that we endure. We come to understand with greater conviction that, in all things, God is drawing us into deeper communion with Himself. As St. Paul understands, *"for those who love God, all things work together for the good"* (Rom 8:28).

Furthermore, by the gift of understanding, we come to appreciate mysteries of our faith that we celebrate in the sacraments. We grasp them as the very action of God accomplishing our salvation. Thus, we recognize in each Eucharist not simply the gathering of the community for worship, but more profoundly the very sacrifice of the Cross made present among us by the power of the Holy Spirit.

As an infused gift of the Holy Spirit, understanding is more than just a *Eureka* moment that comes and then quickly vanishes. It is a habit of mind, not gained by experience, but given as a grace. By it, we have a permanent aptitude to comprehend both supernaturally revealed truths and truths known by reason. It helps us see the connection and unity of God's plan for the world and for ourselves. Thus, the gift of understanding lifts us up beyond this world and ultimately leads us to a deeper union with God in love.

In this world, true understanding among individuals is the basis for peace and charity. Reflecting on forgiveness, the poet Longfellow said, *"If we could read the secret history of our enemies, we would find in each person's life sorrow and suffering enough to disarm all hostility."* By grasping the distress and sufferings that others are enduring, we are moved to compassion and, by our empathy, are united with them. The reverse of this is equally true.

If others could truly understand our feelings, our thoughts, and our suffering, they would be more readily joined to us in charity. Just as we wish to be understood by others, God wills us to understand Him. This is why the Holy Spirit gives us the gift of understanding. As St. Thomas teaches, *"In this very life, when the eye of the spirit is purified by the gift of understanding, one can in a certain way see God"* (*Summa Theologica* II-II, q. 69, a. 2, ad. 3).

At the end of his gospel, St. Luke reports the appearance of the Risen Lord to two disciples on the road to Emmaus (Lk 24:13-35). This event provides an outstanding example of the gift of understanding. Cleopas and another disciple have left Jerusalem. It is toward evening on Easter. They are downcast and confused about the death of Jesus. They simply cannot understand how Jesus came to be crucified if He were truly the Messiah. They were expecting a Messiah Who would liberate them from political oppression. And Jesus did not do this.

The Risen Jesus joins them as they walk, but they do not recognize Him. When Jesus asks them what they are talking about, they relate the events of Jesus' own passion and death. They even tell Him about the discovery of the empty tomb. They have the facts, but they lack understanding. Jesus then gives them a lesson in Scripture. *"Beginning with Moses and all the prophets, he interpreted to them what referred to him in all the scriptures"* (Lk 24:27). He showed them how the events that they had witnessed were part of God's plan already found in the Scriptures.

As Jesus spoke, the truth dawned on them. Once Jesus was gone, *"they said to each other, 'Were not our hearts burning within us while he spoke to us on the way and opened the scriptures to us?'"*(Lk 24:32). As Pope Francis notes, *"mystery enters through the heart"* (Address to Bishops of Brazil, Rio de Janeiro, 2013). Already, on Easter night, on the road to Emmaus, the first disciples are given the gift of understanding. The gift of understanding is never a matter of mere rational explanations. It is, as the Emmaus event shows, a seeing through the heart.

CHAPTER 3

The Gift of Knowledge
The Desire for the Infinite

In the 16th century, at the very time that Michelangelo was painting the Sistine Chapel, Pope Julius II commissioned Raphael to decorate rooms in the Apostolic Palace. The young Raphael took up his work. His first fresco, *The School of Athens*, made a stunning impact on the artists of his day. Greeted with immediate success, the painting is recognized as Raphael's most famous masterpiece.

In this painting, Raphael places twenty-one individuals amid the beauty of classical architecture. The greatest philosophers, mathematicians, and scientists from all different periods of history are seen. He even places the great thinkers and artists of his day. Bramante is shown as Euclid and Leonardo da Vinci as Plato. Seated and resting against a block of marble, Michelangelo appears as Heraclitus. And, from the extreme right of the entire fresco, Raphael himself looks at us.

At the very center of his fresco stand Plato and Aristotle. Both Greek philosophers have influenced Christian thought. Plato stands to the left. He is older and grey with age. He holds in his left hand the *Timaeus*. In this famous work of his, Plato examines the order and beauty in the universe. With his right hand, he points upward. For Plato, ultimate truth, beauty, and goodness are found beyond this world. Plato sees the universe as the handiwork of a divine craftsman working with reason and purpose to create an ordered universe.

In Raphael's fresco, to the right of Plato stands his most distinguished student, Aristotle. A much younger man, he carries in his left hand his universally acclaimed work *Nicomachean Ethics* that explores how best to live life. Looking intently at his teacher, Aristotle points outward, as if to say that truth is found by experiencing the things of this world that can be seen and touched.

Contrasted to earlier artists, Raphael has created a scene that is more than just an allegory of knowledge. His figures are dynamic. They are moving. They engage in discussion, teaching, and learning together.

By placing all these figures engaged in learning in one grandiose architectural framework, Raphael has powerfully expressed the truth that there is within the human spirit a universal thirst for truth. Dedicated to philosophy, *The School of Athens* immortalizes the fact that knowledge of all reality, including the existence of God Who is truth and goodness, can be obtained through the use of human reason meditating on the things of this world.

Ever since Adam and Eve took and ate of the tree of knowledge of good and evil, their descendants have desired to increase their knowledge of this world. Scientists scrutinize the universe to search out its secrets. Historians record and interpret our past so as to enlighten our future. Psychologists delve into the depths of the human psyche to understand our emotions. And, philosophers, with reasoned tranquility, look for ultimate answers.

There is, indeed, a hunger within the soul that only true knowledge can satisfy. Socrates once said, *"The only good is knowledge and the only evil is ignorance."* Plato recognized that *"knowledge is the food of the soul."* Aristotle taught that *"all men by nature desire knowledge.''* The proper object of this universal desire is the truth about things not just theories and opinions. For only true knowledge can lead to the good.

Historically, from the time of the ancient Greek philosophers until the Renaissance, there was a holistic approach to knowledge. But, with the Enlightenment and the divorce of faith from reason, there has been a continual fracturing and fragmentation of knowledge. In today's world of academia, specialists are formed in every field. Our education system provides more and more information on focused and specialized areas of knowledge. Data is generated, passed on, and stored by an ever-accelerating rapidity because of technology. As a result, *"in the past 150 years, we have lost not only the possibility of broad and integrated knowledge, we have lost even the myth of it"* (Steven B. Sample, "The Great Straddlers as Successor to the Renaissance Man," March 13, 1993).

We are constantly exposed today to a rationalistic and fragmented understanding of reality. As a result, we may be tempted to simply accept a naturalistic interpretation to the world. We run the risk of making the things of this world, e.g., possessions, pleasure, and power, the very purpose of our lives. To help us avoid this temptation and rightly judge created reality, the Holy Spirit gives us the gift of knowledge.

In his loving providence, God has created all things that exist. As St. Thomas Aquinas teaches, *"God brought things into being in order that his goodness might be communicated to creatures and be represented by them.... For goodness, which in God is simple and uniform, in creatures is manifold and divided"* (Thomas Aquinas, *Summa Theologica*, I, 47, 1). Thus, everything that God has made reflects, in one way or another, His Truth, His Goodness, and His Beauty and can lead us to God. By the gift of knowledge, we recognize the perfection of God in the things of this world and are led to praise Him.

The gift of knowledge helps us value things correctly. We see all created realities in their essential dependence on the Creator. We do not give more value to creatures than they deserve. And, we certainly do not make them the purpose of our lives. Only God is! (see St. Thomas Aquinas, *Summa Theologica*, II-II, q. 9, a. 4). In a word, the Holy Spirit enables us to see all created things in relation to God.

The gift of knowledge is not the end product of a laborious reasoning process. It is not something learned in school. The gift of knowledge moves our intellect by a divine impulse. Knowledge allows us to make the right judgments about the things of this world. The gift of knowledge helps us judge rightly not only things, but the circumstances and events. In a limited way, it allows us to see God's purpose in our lives.

On the one hand, it makes us appreciate creation. We see the goodness, the beauty, and the truth of created things as coming from God. We see *"the infinite distance which separates things from the Creator, their intrinsic limitation, the danger that they can present, when, through sin, [we make] improper use of them. It is a discovery which leads [us] to realize with remorse [our] misery and impels [us]to turn with greater drive and confidence to Him who alone can fully satisfy the need of the infinite..."*(Pope St. John Paul II, *Regina Coeli*, April 23, 1989).

On the other hand, the gift of knowledge enables us to be detached from this world. We recognize that things cannot bring us the ultimate happiness that comes from God alone. Thus, we do not stumble on the things of this world. They are no longer obstacles in our journey to God. Rather, we use them as stepping stones to draw closer to God who loves us so much as to give us all the good things of this world. We see *"things as true and real, although limited, manifestations of the Truth, Beauty, and infinite Love which is God, and consequently [we feel] impelled to translate this discovery into praise, song, prayer, and thanksgiving"* (*ibid*).

CHAPTER 4

The Gift of Counsel
A Guide to the Present

Horoscopes, tarot cards, palm-reading, astrology, and tasseography (reading patterns in coffee grounds, tea leaves, or wine sediment left in an empty cup) remain as popular today as reading the entrails of animals in the days of ancient Rome. Fortune-telling, in one way or another, is as old as the human race. From kings to paupers, people have always had the desire to know what lies in the future, whether weal or woe, so that they make the right decisions.

No doubt the most famous of all places to consult about the future was the ancient shrine of the Oracle of Delphi in Greece. Located on Mt. Parnassus near the Gulf of Corinth, this sanctuary had a widespread popularity. Delphi owed its popularity to human nature itself. People always want the right advice to guide their lives to success. The ancient people of the Mediterranean were no different. They made no major decision without first consulting the Oracle of Delphi.

At Delphi, the Pythia, or priestess of Apollo, would answer questions on anything from the time to go to war to the time for a farmer to plant his crops. Rulers and common folk, heads of state, and ordinary farmers, Greeks and foreigners made their pilgrimage to this sanctuary. Devotees were always willing to pay a great price to peer into the future. States would even shower the sanctuary with rich gifts to keep the favor of the Oracle. Eventually, the spread of Christianity reduced Delphi to an archaeological ruin. Apollo was no match for Christ.

The Christian faith has no room for fortune-telling. Nor does it allow a place for manipulating the future for one's own good. God is in control of His creation. Not stars. Not devils. Not tea leaves. At the heart of faith is the act of trust in the wise providence of an all-loving God. Trust in God casts out worry and anxiety about the future. As Jesus teaches in the Sermon on the Mount, *"So do not worry and say, 'What are we to eat?' or 'What are we to drink?' or 'What are we to wear?' All these things the pagans seek. Your heavenly Father knows that you need them all. But seek first the kingdom of God and his righteousness, and all these things will be given you besides"* (Mt 6:31-33).

When someone turns to any form of fortune-telling or divination, they are actually doubting the goodness of God and trusting in forces other than God Himself to direct their decisions. *"In order to solve their problems many people resort to fortune tellers and tarot cards. But only Jesus saves, and we must bear witness to this! He is the only one"* (Pope Francis, Morning Mass at *Domus Sanctae Marthae*, April 5, 2013). Our curiosity about the future should never deter us from trusting in the Lord. As St. Paul reminds us, *"God makes all things work together for the good of those who love him, who have been called according to his decree"* (Rom 8:28). And, He offers us the gift of His counsel to help us choose the good that He wills for our happiness.

In the Old Testament times, God gave His prophets the counsel which they needed to guide His people. As Amos announced to the people of the northern kingdom of Israel, *"the Lord God does nothing without revealing his plan to his servants the prophets"* (Am 3:7). At the time of the Babylonian exile,

Jeremiah separated himself from those who did not know God's plan for the nation.

In the sixth century before Christ, false prophets were promising peace and security in the face of an imminent invasion from Babylon. However, Jeremiah was predicting punishment for the sins of the nation. Jeremiah warns against these shalom prophets. He says, *"Do not listen to the words of your prophets, who fill you with emptiness. They speak visions from their own fancy, not from the mouth of the Lord"* (Jer 23:16). Jeremiah exposes their credentials as false by telling the people that these prophets have not stood in the council of the Lord. They did not see Him. They did not hear His word (see Jer 23:18). Standing in "the council of the Lord" distinguishes the true prophet from the false.

In his dramatic confrontation with Ahab, the king of the northern kingdom of Israel, the ninth century prophet Micaiah ben Imlah vividly describes "the council of the Lord." Ahab has already initiated a plan to recapture Ramoth-gilead. This Levitical city of refuge was strategically located east of the Jordan. The Syrians had captured this frontier city and Ahab was determined to take it back.

After making his plans, Ahab invites Jehoshaphat, the king of the southern kingdom of Judah to join with him in his military campaign. Though on friendly terms with each other, the two kings differ greatly. Together with his ruthless wife Jezebel, Ahab had corrupted the northern kingdom with the worship of false gods. However, Jehoshaphat had banished idolatry from Judah. Deep was his piety and strong his influence in wiping out false worship in his kingdom and in promoting strict adherence to the Torah among his subjects.

Thus, when Ahab puts his proposal for war before him, Jehoshaphat does not agree until they both seek the counsel of the Lord. This should have been done before, and not after, the decision to go to war had been made. With those who have no faith, God is never a factor in formulating their plans. But, with those with faith, no area of life is outside of God's wise providence.

Simply to satisfy Jehoshaphat, the less scrupulous Ahab summons to court four hundred of the prophets of Baal. With one voice, they approved his plans. Truth does not concern them. Principle matters little. They fear displeasing the king to whom they owe their livelihood. They tell the king what he wants to hear. They act out of human respect.

It is a natural desire to want to please those above us and those around us. But, when we curry the favor of others in small things, we will end surrendering our principles in great matters. It is better to incur the displeasure of others by telling the truth than to lose one's integrity by pleasing them with a lie. Each day, we face the stark choice between seeking the approval of God and winning the approval of others. Our sinful nature inclines us to make those choices that put us in harmony with the City of Man, while God is constantly gifting us with his grace to live as good citizens of the City of God. The choice is ours.

According to Flavius Josephus, the Jewish historian, when Ahab's prophets spoke, Jehoshaphat understood from their language that they were false prophets. Immediately he asks for a prophet of the Lord to be consulted. Micaiah, the son of Imlah, was then summoned to court. One faithful prophet of the Lord was worth more than four hundred flattering charlatans. But, Ahab abhorred Micaiah. At the very mention of his name, he erupts into anger. He accuses him of only prophesying evil. He even suggests to Jehoshaphat that he puts forth his personal opinions as if they were oracles from on high.

In this context where the prophet's credentials are being questioned, Micaiah explains the origin of his prophetic utterances. He says, *"I saw the Lord seated on his throne, with the whole host of heaven standing to his right and to his left. The Lord asked: 'Who will deceive Ahab, so that he will go up and fall on Ramoth-gilead?' And one said this, another that, until this spirit came forth and stood before the Lord, saying, 'I will deceive him.' The Lord asked: 'How?' He answered, 'I will go forth and become a lying spirit in the mouths of all his prophets.' The Lord replied: 'You shall succeed in deceiving him. Go forth and do this.' So now, the Lord has put a lying spirit in the mouths of all these prophets of yours; the Lord himself has decreed evil against you"* (1 Kgs 22:19-23).

In this vision of Micaiah, God appears as the king seated on his throne. God is holding court, surrounded by the gods of the pagan nations who do His bidding. As God ponders the fate of Ahab with his court, the prophet himself is admitted into the meeting of the heavenly council. Thus, the true prophet is the one who stands in the midst of the council *(sodh)* of God from which issues forth God's counsel *(sodh)*, that is, God's advice.

Ahab does not heed the counsel of God given by Micaiah. Obstinate individuals are rarely strong enough to change their minds when reason urges and faith demands. Ahab disguises himself and goes to battle at Ramoth-gilead. A man, riding in his chariot, shoots his arrow and, without knowing it, kills the king. So easily do the enemies of God perish!

David killed Goliath with a pebble. A nameless warrior brings down the proud and stubborn king of Israel. No armor protects those who turn their back on God's gifts. Disgrace adds ignominy to his death. The Hebrew Scriptures say that the dogs licked his blood. The Septuagint (the Greek translation of the Old Testament) adds further insult by saying that pigs also licked his blood. There was no other animal more loathsome to the pious Israelite.

God is patient. He wants no one to perish. He wants all to repent, to change their minds and hearts, and live in accord with His plan, His counsel (see 2 Pt 3:9). He loves us too much to take away a freedom. With the gift of counsel, He shows what is best for our eternal happiness. With the gentle presence of the Holy Spirit, He moves our conscience to recognize what is right for us to do (St. Bonaventure, *Collationes de septem donis Spiritus Sancti,* VII, 5). In this way, we see more clearly what is best to do in any situation, no matter how complicated and confusing.

God does not leave us alone. He is always present to us, helping, and guiding us. At the Last Supper, Jesus promised us the Holy Spirit. He said, *"I will ask the Father, and he will give you another Advocate to be with you always, the Spirit of truth... I will not leave you orphans"* (Jn 14:16-18). The Holy Spirit is our Advocate. The English word "advocate" translates the Greek *parakletos* in this passage. It comes from the common Greek verb *parakalein*. Often used in a legal context, this verb means to speak in support of something as an advocate in a defense case. It also means to exhort or to urge.

Again and again, the verb *parakalein* is the word of the rallying call. It is the action of leaders who urge their soldiers on to battle. A "paraclete" is the one who puts courage in the faint-hearted and makes the ordinary person struggle valiantly in battle, as Xenophon of Athens did with his troops when they joined in Cyrus of Persia's attempt to regain his throne.

As "the Paraclete," the Holy Spirit guides, advises, consoles, and urges us on in our daily struggle to be faithful followers of Jesus. The Holy Spirit is always at our side to give us counsel. He is our Counselor who leads us into all truth (see Jn 16:13).

The Holy Spirit's gift of counsel does not exempt us from exercising the natural virtue of prudence. Prudence is that common sense understanding about our lives that moves us to make the appropriate choice for a given moment and place. It lets us use our reason to judge what actions are good and what actions are evil, not just in general, but in particular. In the concrete circumstances of our lives, prudence shows us the golden mean that is at the heart of all natural virtues. Without prudence, courage becomes foolhardiness and mercy is simply forbearance.

With His gentle presence within us, the Holy Spirit brings the natural virtue of prudence to a supernatural level with His gift of counsel. The gift of counsel is, as St. Thomas Aquinas describes it, *"the perfection of prudence."* It elevates that clear-sighted ability to understand what is happening in our lives and to act sensibly in light of that new understanding. It makes it easy for us to make judgments promptly in light of our supernatural destiny.

The Holy Spirit's gift of counsel embraces every aspect of our lives—for nothing is outside the wise providence of God. The gift of counsel does not provide us with a specific answer to our question about what will happen to us in the future. No! It is the guidance given at a particular moment about how to live a life of goodness in the present.

Parents, teachers, students, children, young adults, and public servants each day face a round of choices between good and evil. In many instances, the choice is not so clear. Through the gift of counsel, the Holy Spirit helps us discern the good from the evil. The gift does not give us a ready-made answer. Rather, with His gift of counsel, the Holy Spirit stirs up within us an attraction to what is the appropriate thing to do and a repugnance to what is sinful. It assures us, in times of joy and suffering, in favorable and adverse moments, that we are acting correctly for our own salvation and the glory of God.

In the Bible, King Solomon is remembered as the wisest man of all time. In his own day, he attracted many important dignitaries to visit him. He himself gives the secret of his ability to govern with such success. He says, *"With many advisors, there is success"* (Prv 24:6). Good leaders are willing to listen to others. They are humble enough to know that they do not know everything. They are ready to heed the advice of those who are more knowledgeable. We do not need to travel to distant places such as Delphi or to soothsayers close at hand to find the best advisor. Through Baptism and Confirmation, the Holy Spirit dwells within us. When we open our hearts and are ready to follow the Holy Spirit prompting us with His gift of counsel, we come to possess an intuitive, supernatural common sense to guide us. What a priceless treasure in our search for true happiness!

CHAPTER 5

The Gift of Fortitude
The Victory over Fear

In the annals of history, our time will be remembered as the return of the age of martyrs. For the first three hundred years of Christianity, Christians courageously faced death rather than deny their faith. A quick survey of the vast expanse of the Church's entire history, however, reveals the astonishing fact that sixty-five percent of all martyrs belong to our time. As Pope St. John Paul II wrote, *"In our own century, the martyrs have returned, many of them nameless, unknown soldiers as it were of God's great cause"* (*Tertio Millennio Ineunte*, 37).

Many people live in places where local governments, social groups, or individuals restrict people's ability to freely practice their faith. In countries where there are open hostilities against Christians, new restrictions on religion come as no shock. But, sadly, there is surprise and dismay when other countries such as Switzerland and the United States move in the direction of restricting the practice of religion.

In no country today can faithful Christians avoid either persecution for the faith or hostility towards it. Sometimes it is open; sometimes, subtle. Christians simply cannot escape today's challenge to be a martyr, that is, a witness to the faith. Some are called to the ultimate witness of giving their lives for the sake of the Gospel. All of us are called to live in clear witness to the faith. In both instances, the virtue of fortitude is needed.

In the midst of today's daunting challenges, God does not abandon us. He strengthens us in our weakness. He enlightens our intellect so that we know and understand what is morally good. He supports us, sustains us, and strengthens us with fortitude, one of the seven gifts of the Holy Spirit. This gift enables us to do what is morally right despite any opposition.

When we face threats to our well-being or obstacles to block our good deeds, fortitude helps us overcome fear and allows us to act. It is the courage to live the Christian faith in its fullness, despite the hostility and derision that we face. Fortitude is not fearlessness. It is *"not the absence of fear, but the triumph over it. The brave man is not he who does not feel afraid, but he who conquers that fear"*

(Nelson Mandela). The Christian conquers fear through the power of the Holy Spirit.

Examples of courage crowd the pages of Sacred Scripture. Moses against Pharaoh. David against Goliath. Daniel in the lions' den. Esther before the Persian king Ahasuerus. Stephen at his stoning. Peter and John before the Sanhedrin. Paul before Festus. The list could continue. History, too, does not lack its canon of martyrs for the truth. Thomas More before the English Parliament. Edith Stein before the Nazis. Rosa Parks on a Montgomery bus. Oscar Romero at the altar. Martin Luther King, Jr., in his pulpit. Some individuals accept death as the price of their fidelity to the truth. Others are called to live their lives in witness to the truth. In every one of them, fortitude is at work.

One very remarkable biblical figure of fortitude is Deborah. She lived in the twelfth century before Christ. The Bible first introduces us to Deborah as a prophetess (see Jgs 4:4). In this role, she takes her place alongside of Moses' sister Miriam (see Ex 15:20), the wife of the prophet Isaiah (see Is 8:3) and Huldah (see 2 Kgs 22:14). In a culture ruled by men, these women had a major role to play in the history of God's people during Old Testament times.

Likewise, in New Testament times, women had a significant impact on the spiritual life of the early Church. Priscilla was a valued co-worker of Paul in the ministry (see Rom 16:3). The four daughters of Philip the deacon were prophetesses (see Acts 21:9). Chloe was the apparent leader of a house church at Corinth (see 1 Cor 1:11).

Then, there was Junia. Paul praises her as *"prominent among the apostles"* (Rom 16:7). For some in later generations, this simply could not be: Junia, a woman, listed among the apostles. So, in the thirteenth century, Aegidius of Rome changed "Junia" (a woman's name) into "Junias" (a man's name). He was followed by other biblical translators who recoiled from listing a woman as an apostle. But, both in Old Testament and New Testament times, God did call into His service women of great virtue. And He still does today. From among all these women, Deborah stands out as a model of courage.

When God enlisted Deborah in His service, the Chosen People had been living in the Promised Land for a hundred years. After the conquest of Canaan until Saul was anointed king, the twelve tribes of Israel functioned as a loose confederation. In times of crisis that required a more stable unity, God raised up charismatic leaders to deliver His people from danger. These ad hoc leaders were called "judges." They could trace their role back to the assistants Moses appointed to help him resolve disputes among the people (see Ex 18).

At the time of Deborah, Israel was weak and fearful. Jabin, king of Hazor, had subjugated the nation under the cruel yoke of the Canaanites for twenty years. The people were dejected. Their hope of deliverance, gone. Patriotism dead. The Israelites had lapsed into the worship of false gods and were reaping the harvest of their sins.

In the hill country of Ephraim, Deborah was quite a familiar person. She would sit under a palm tree, ready to dispense justice (see Jgs 4:5). Men and women gladly came to receive her counsel. To her human intuition was added divine inspiration. In Deborah, faith and reason join together in attaining truth. As Pope St. John Paul II taught, *"Faith and reason are like two wings on which the human spirit rises to the contemplation of truth..."* *(Fides et Ratio, 1).*

Unfortunately, within our academic institutions and within our secular culture, faith and reason have been divorced. But, science and religion are not enemies.

God has gifted us with reason. The rational search for truth, done in charity, will always lead to the Truth Who alone can bring us lasting happiness. As Catholics, we are heirs to a vast intellectual search for truth in every science. Galileo, the father of modern science; Copernicus, first to formulate a comprehensive heliocentric cosmology; Descartes, father of modern philosophy; the monk Mendel, the father of genetics; Pasteur, founder of bacteriology; and, the priest, Lemaître, the father of the Big Bang Theory; just to name a few. Our faith does not destroy reason. It guides and directs it, like a light shining through a fog.

Faith opens our minds to God Who is never absent from His world. Faith enables our hearts to hear His voice in the circumstances of our lives. Thus, when the Israelites brought to Deborah the cruel sufferings inflicted on them by the Canaanites, she saw beyond Jabin's army. She saw God's plan for deliverance. She heard Him speak to her and she acted.

Deborah summoned Barak, the general of Israel's army. She informed him that God wanted him to deliver the country from the scourge of the powerful Canaanites. But, Barak hesitated. There had been many failed attempts. The enemy was too powerful. Barak had only 10,000 men to go to war with him against Sisera who commanded 10,000 men and 900 iron chariots.

Deborah was not deterred. She ordered Barak to go to the foot of Mt. Tabor and engage in battle. This seasoned soldier, so timid and fearful, objected. Barak was a military commander who had the skills and experience of war. But he lacked a clear understanding of God's plan and purpose. Deborah provided both.

Deborah did not yield to Barak's fear. Her courage in the face of danger elicited from Barak one of the most unusual responses of Scripture. Barak answered Deborah, *"If you will go with me, I will go; if not, I will not go"* (Jgs 4:8). Barak, a man, confessed his dependence on a woman. His response shows the great esteem in which all the people held Deborah. Wasting no time, *"Deborah arose and went with Barak"* (Jgs 4:9). The battle began.

It was the rainy season in Israel, somewhere between October and December. The heavens opened and poured their wrath on the enemies of God's people. A hailstorm blinded their soldiers. The river Kishon, swollen with rain, turned the battlefield into a muddy swamp. The heavy chariots of the Canaanites were paralyzed. An easy prey for Israel. Israel won the battle.

God had come to the aid of His people. He used the forces of nature to favor his people. He used the courage of Deborah to rouse them to action. No other woman in Israel ever rose to the height of military power. No other woman in the Bible stands out in bolder relief as a model of fortitude. Where men stumbled in fear, she boldly led the way.

In the time of Deborah, God's people had to fight against the oppression of their idolatrous neighbors who were corrupting their faith. Today, God's people are engaged in a powerful struggle against those who would rob them of the practice of their faith. When confronted with evil that seems insurmountable, it is always tempting to respond, like Barak, with pessimism, indifference or skepticism. It is the Holy Spirit's gift of fortitude that strengthens us in the fight for freedom to live our faith in peace.

Today's secularistic mindset holds that no religious consideration should enter into the affairs of state, government, or public education. Many university professors, judges, and legislators actively promote the secularization of our society. They zealously work to remove any vestige of Judeo-Christian morality from the public square. Believers need fortitude not just to resist but to transform this secularistic mindset.

In an age of secularism, life is a laboratory in which we are set free to experiment with different ideas and values. A culture that rejects God, constantly offers alcohol, drugs, and sex as ways to liberate the individual from all moral restraints. For the timid, it is simply easier to go along with everyone else. It takes fortitude to stand on one's own. *"To be yourself in a world that is constantly trying to make you something else is the greatest accomplishment"* (Ralph Waldo Emerson).

Living in a society that confronts us with the inescapable diversity of beliefs, worldviews, lifestyles, and moral choices, we are always to be tolerant. Some define tolerance as accepting the convictions of others as true as our own. However, this is not tolerance. It is acquiescence.

Tolerance means that we live with others in mutual respect and understanding. We shun being judgmental of others. But, this hardly means that, in the name of tolerance, we do not exercise any moral judgment at all. Our culture's deifying of tolerance cannot demonize us when we have the courage to stand up for moral principles and the fortitude to live according to them. The true and the good can never be compromised if we are to have a life that is truly beautiful.

The first Christians had to struggle against the pagan culture in which they lived. Their moral values were at variance with those fostered by the state. Abortion and infanticide were widely practiced among every class of people. A woman was subject to her father and then to her husband. She had no legal identity. No woman could vote or hold public office. Freeborn men were expected to have extramarital sex both with female and male partners, as long as they confined their sexual activity to slaves, prostitutes, or concubines. Divorce was widely accepted.

As Christianity spread, believers rejected these practices on the basis of the gospel. Children were accepted even when born ill. Chastity was promoted. Marriage between a man and a woman upheld. And, the status of women gradually improved. Because individual believers courageously lived out their beliefs, faith impacted public life for the betterment of society as a whole, making it more civil and more humane. No less fortitude is required of us today.

Fortitude is not the reckless abandon to expose oneself to danger or to death. Not at all. It is the reasoned courage to stand up for the truth, justice, the dignity of the human person, and the common good. It is the moral virtue that enables us to follow our rightly formed conscience, come what may. With the virtue of fortitude given to us by the Holy Spirit, we can readily face danger, resolutely accept hardship, and gladly suffer loss for the good of others. Those gifted with the virtue of fortitude love God and neighbor more than themselves. Morally courageous individuals are never selfish.

Although most of us may never be called to exercise the virtue of fortitude in a dramatic way, nonetheless, we are being called to exercise this virtue in the choices we make each day. As we live our faith and the moral teachings of Jesus, we face opposition and persecution. Fortitude makes us courageous enough to rise above apathy and complacency. It puts us on the path to action in face of the dangers that lie ahead. It does not make us shrink from the risk of marginalization, unpopularity and, even at times, the loss of a job or promotion.

Moral courage does not always roar. It is sometimes the gentle voice of conscience that makes us stand against the evils of our day. Many today advocate and agitate for radical social changes that clearly oppose the teaching of Jesus. As His faithful followers, we must speak the truth, uphold the dignity of each person, whether poor or rich, healthy or ill. We must defend life from the moment of conception in the womb of a mother to the moment of natural death. We must embrace God's plan for marriage and family life and stand for honesty in business, justice in politics, and chastity in society. These are polarizing issues in our day. In some cases, *"There are no easy answers but there are simple answers. We must have the*

courage to do what we know is morally right"
(Ronald Reagan).

Fortitude empowers us to speak, even if our voice trembles. It enables us to act, even if alone. Fortitude does not guarantee that we will be successful at all times. But it does enable us to be faithful and courageous enough to stand against evil. And such moral courage is already the Holy Spirit's victory over our fearful self.

CHAPTER 6
The Gift of Piety
True Loyalty to God and to Neighbor

Inside St. Peter's Basilica in the Vatican, to the right of the main entrance, stands Michelangelo's *Pietà*. The *Pietà* quietly draws the viewer into the profound grief that Mary experienced at the death of her only son. Holding the lifeless body of Jesus on her lap, Mary looks with deep affection on the child she gave to the world to be its savior. With outstretched left hand, she beckons the viewer to share her own sentiments of love and devotion to Jesus.

Michelangelo's Renaissance masterpiece memorializes in marble the virtue of piety. No surprise that Michelangelo would choose piety as the subject of the world's most famous religious sculpture. The ancient Romans, whose art and culture were at the heart of the Renaissance, placed great value on piety.

For some, the noun "piety" and the adjective "pious" may suggest a saccharine disposition or an unctuous attitude. It conjures up images of an overly excessive religiosity or a sentimental superficiality in matters of religion. Some may even make the mistake of equating piety with hypocrisy. But, this is to misunderstand the real meaning of piety as a virtue.

The ancient Romans traditionally understood piety as taking one's responsibilities seriously. A pious individual was the person who fulfilled all of his or her duties to the gods and to others. At the time that the Roman Republic was in its decline, the great philosopher and orator Cicero said, *"Piety is justice toward the gods and the foundation of all virtues" (De Natura Deorum 1.116).* He also said that piety *"admonishes us to do our duty to our country or our parents or other blood relations" (De inventione 2.22.66).* Piety was both a religious and social virtue. So it likewise is in Sacred Scripture.

On the one hand, Psalm 119 exemplifies piety as a religious virtue. This psalm, the longest in the psalter, extols God's law. Each verse contains a special word for the law, e.g., ordinances, word, commandments, statutes, precepts, and decrees. The psalm makes clear that the truly good person, the pious individual, delights to do God's will because his or her own desire and prayer is to do what God commands. This psalm captures the essence of Hebrew piety in terms of God. Piety is reverencing and respecting God, keeping His commandments not out of a sense of fear or dread, not as a heavy burden, but as a joyful response to God Who wants what it is best for us.

On the other hand, the book of Ruth epitomizes piety as a social virtue. Ruth, a woman from Moab, marries the son of Naomi from Bethlehem. Ruth's husband dies as well as his brother, and their widowed mother Naomi is left alone. Ruth remains steadfast in her love and care of her mother-in-law. When Naomi is about to return to her home in Judah, Ruth tells Naomi, *"Wherever you go I will go, wherever you lodge I will lodge. Your people shall be my people and your God, my God"* (Ru 1:16). For the Hebrews, this is true filial piety. Ruth remains devoted and loyal to family. Ruth's piety is so blessed by God that she, a foreigner, becomes the great-grandmother of David, from whose line the Messiah is born.

Michelangelo's *Pietà* captures both the religious and the social dimension of piety. Mary tenderly holds the body of the Crucified Jesus. No trace of rebellion, no sign of anger across her face. Her serene countenance betrays her total acquiescence to the will of God. Her Son was obedient to the Father's will, accepting death on the Cross for our salvation. Mary, likewise, is obedient to God's will, even as the sword of sorrow pierces her maternal heart.

Furthermore, Mary is with Jesus to the bitter end. From the crib to the Cross, Mary was always at the side of her Son, supporting Him and loving Him. She is present to Him throughout His public ministry. Nothing was ever able to keep her apart from the child that God had given into her care. From Cana to Calvary, Mary is there loving her Son. And, Jesus himself returned her great love. In His last moments, He cares for His mother, entrusting her to John, the Beloved Apostle. Never abandoning one's own: is this not the greatest example of duty and responsibility within a family? This is true piety.

The pages of Scripture are crowded with other pious individuals who are steadfast in loving obedience to God and attentive to the needs of others. Abraham is willing to sacrifice his son Isaac in obedience to God. Joseph refuses to do anything that offends God grievously. Simeon and Anna prayerfully await the Messiah. Mary Magdalene is the first to visit the tomb of Jesus. Tabitha, the wealthy disciple, attends the needs of the poor at Joppa. Each of these, with unselfish hearts and great joy, are devoted to God and to neighbor.

Piety is one of the seven gifts given by the Holy Spirit at Baptism and Confirmation. As an infused gift, it is a disposition or attitude that helps us follow the inspirations of the Holy Spirit (see *Catechism of the Catholic Church*, 1830-1831). This divinely given gift nourishes sentiments of profound confidence in God and His will for us. It moves us to works of mercy and compassion toward others.

Piety makes it easier for us to trust God, even when we do not understand His will. Piety opens the way for us to live our ordinary life in intimacy with God. Piety prompts us to pray. It allows us to be held in God's loving embrace. Moved by the gift of piety, we live our lives as a continual conversation with God. Not just our words but our deeds and our silence become a prayer. Piety helps us pray without ceasing, just as Paul tells us to do in 1 Thessalonians 5:17. And, when we pray without ceasing, we always have a reason to be thankful. In pleasant and prosperous moments, we are grateful for God's gifts. In trials and deprivations, we rejoice in His providence. The truly pious individual remains united with God in heart and mind.

Furthermore, as a gift of the Holy Spirit, piety helps us to respect and love others with practical charity, coming to assist them in their need. We see others as children of God. We recognize them as part of the family of God to which we belong. We feel urged to treat all *"with the kindness and friendliness which are proper to a frank and fraternal relationship ... [Piety] is at the root of that new human community, which is based on the civilization of love"* (Pope St. John Paul II, *Angelus,* May 14, 1989).

Reverencing and obeying God in all things and remaining steadfast in prayer can be difficult and painful. Remaining united with family members and assisting those in need is not always easy. But the gift of piety enables us to be unswerving in our devotion to God and one another. Where we may be tempted to fail, the Holy Spirit strengthens us with this gift. The heart of true piety is unshakable loyalty, so clearly seen in Jesus and Mary in the Passion.

CHAPTER 7

The Fear of the Lord
Joy-filled Awe in the
Presence of God

Fear is an emotion that hardly seems desirable! At least, that is what most people think. Francis Bacon once said, *"Nothing is terrible except fear itself."* Edmund Burke believed that *"no passion so effectually robs the mind of all its powers of acting and reasoning as fear."* And, Ralph Waldo Emerson observed that *"fear defeats more people than any other one thing in the world."*

Because of this negative understanding of fear as a disabling emotion, many people reckon fear a detriment to our relationship with God. Some would banish the very mention of fear of the Lord from any liturgical text. Others would exorcize it completely from our religious vocabulary. How could we possibly speak of fear in approaching a God Who loves us so much? After all, does not Sacred Scripture itself say that *"God has not given us a spirit of fear but of power and of love and of a sound mind"* (2 Tm 1:7)?

The great Greek philosopher Aristotle defined fear as a pain arising from the anticipation of evil. He said that *"fear is caused by whatever we feel has great power of destroying us, or of harming us in ways that tend to cause us great pain"* (see Aristotle, *Rhetoric*, Book II, chapter 5). For Aristotle, fear is opposed to love. Thus, he concluded that *"no one loves the man whom he fears."*

Yet, contrary to this understanding, Sacred Scripture tells us that the God whom we are to love, we are told also to fear. *"Now, therefore,…what does the Lord, your God, ask of you but to fear the Lord, your God, to follow in all his ways, to love and serve the Lord, your God, with your whole heart and with your whole being"* (Dt 10:12). In defining our relationship with God, Deuteronomy places fear of the Lord first. And, not by accident.

At least three hundred times, Sacred Scripture uses the word "fear" in reference to God. In Genesis 22, the idea of the fear of God, not as dreading God, but as reverencing and obeying Him, is found for the first time. The aging patriarch Abraham is commanded to sacrifice his only son Isaac. For Abraham, this means the end of the promise that he would be father of a great people with progeny as numerous as the sands on the seashore (see Gn 32:12). But, at the very moment when Abraham is about to do as he has been commanded, the angel of the Lord stays his hand with these words: *"Do not lay your hand on the boy or do anything to him, for now I know that you fear God, since you have not withheld your son"* (Gn 22:12). In this instance, fear means obedience, not slavish or feudal, but filial obedience. It is the obedience of faith that stands in awe of God and trusts God, Who is always beyond our human understanding.

When the patriarch Joseph wishes his brothers to know that he would do them no harm, he assures them that he fears God (see Gn 42:18). When a violent storm threatens to destroy the ship on which the prophet Jonah is traveling, the sailors question his goodness. He responds by saying, *"I fear the Lord, the God of heaven, who made the sea and dry land"* (Jon 1:9). Both Joseph and Jonah stand in awe and reverence before the will of God. They are to be trusted.

Nehemiah was the governor of the Jews when they returned to their land after the Babylonian Captivity. He describes himself as a man who desires to fear God (see Neh 1:11). In other words, he holds God as the *"great and awesome God"* (Neh 1:5; 4:14). He has nothing but the highest respect and reverence for Him.

In the events leading up to the Exodus, Pharaoh commands the Hebrew midwives to kill all newborn Hebrew boys. But, instead, they spare the boys' lives. Because the midwives fear God, they disobey the unjust civil authority (see Ex 1:17-20). Fear of the Lord is not an emotion. It is the acknowledgment by word and deed that the world is in the hands of God.

The author of Psalm 111, like the author of Proverbs, highly values the fear of the Lord as an incentive to a righteous walk with God (see Ps 111:10; Prv 9:10). Qoheleth goes as far as to sum up our entire relationship with God by saying, *"The last word, when all is heard: Fear God and keep his commandments, for this is man's all"* (Qo 12:13). In twenty-seven places, the Bible directly commends the fear of the Lord as something positive, helpful, and enabling.

The biblical understanding of fear, therefore, is much different than the one we find among philosophers and in common use.

Its meaning is rich and varied. The Hebrew word *yirah* (fear) means more than the feeling of dread or anxious anticipation in the face of danger. It includes reverence, wonder, awe, amazement, astonishment, and even worship. Some Jewish sages make an etymological link between the word *yirah* (fear) and the word *ra'ah* (seeing). For them, seeing reality as it truly is means being filled with fear, that is, overcome with wonder and with awe.

When we truly fear the Lord, we stand in awe of His mystery, and realize, as Abraham Heschel has said, *"that things not only are what they are but also stand, however remotely, for something supreme. . . .It enables us to perceive in the world intimations of the divine, to sense in small things the beginning of infinite significance, to sense the ultimate in the common and the simple, to feel in the rush of the passing the stillness of the eternal. What we cannot comprehend by analysis, we become aware of in awe"* (Abraham Heschel, *Who Is Man?*, Chapter 5).

The Scriptures affirm that this awe, this reverence, this fear of the Lord, is one of the seven gifts of the Holy Spirit (Is 11:2-3). They understand it as the beginning of wisdom (see Prv 1:7; 9:10; 10:27; Ps 111:10). It is not the beginning in the sense that, once we progress in our relationship with God, fear gives way to love. Not at all!

The fear of the Lord is the beginning of any authentic relationship with God in the same sense that conception is the beginning of life. We begin to live as a person the moment we are conceived in our mother's womb. But our life does not end when we are born. We need to grow and mature. In the same way, fear of the Lord is the beginning, the starting point, the foundation of a right relationship with God. This right relationship needs to grow and mature and will only reach its full measure in heaven where our hearts will be bursting with joy. In the court of heaven, we will be overwhelmed with awe and wonder before the divine majesty of God. Amazed, astonished by His love, we will truly understand that *"the fear of the Lord…endures forever"* (Ps 19:10).

The concept of the fear of the Lord is deeply biblical. Thus, to delete the scriptural expression "the fear of the Lord" from liturgy and catechesis would be to impoverish our understanding of a fundamental truth of our relationship with God. On the other hand, using the expression "the fear of the Lord" means safeguarding and handing on the language of faith that we inherit from the Word of God itself. The very use of the expression "the fear of the Lord" helps to move beyond too simplistic and overly rational explanations of our relationship with God. It directs our minds and hearts to the very mystery of our loving God Who leaves us in awe and wonder before His ineffable presence.

Conclusion

Jesus, the Son of David, was anointed by the Holy Spirit to accomplish His Messianic mission as Savior of the world. The Holy Spirit poured out on His humanity the seven gifts of wisdom, understanding, counsel, fortitude, knowledge, piety, and fear of the Lord in their fullness. As crucified and risen from the dead, the Lord Jesus shares these very same gifts with all believers. First given us in Baptism and then more fully in Confirmation, these gifts help us to respond to the presence of the Holy Spirit in our lives, to make good choices, to serve God and others, and to walk the path that leads to eternal happiness.

Jesus began His public ministry with the call to conversion, *"This is the time of fulfillment. The kingdom of God is at hand. Repent, and believe in the gospel"* (Mk 1:15). By blessing us with His seven gifts, the Holy Spirit enables us to respond to Jesus' invitation. As St. Thomas Aquinas teaches, wisdom, understanding, knowledge, and counsel influence and direct our intellect. These four gifts help us understand and recognize the kingdom of God in our midst. The other three gifts, fortitude, piety, and fear of the Lord, touch our will, enabling us to repent, turning away from all sin to God.

With His seven gifts, the Holy Spirit accompanies us throughout our whole life. He is there every moment of our lives. When we live in the state of grace, that is, free from mortal sin, He is present to us, helping us with these gifts to grow in holiness and to be more perfectly united to Christ Who alone can fulfill our deepest longings.

The Father is ever ready to bestow the gifts of the Holy Spirit on us when we turn to Him in silence and prayer. *"For everyone who asks, receives; and the one who seeks, finds; and to the one who knocks, the door will be opened... your heavenly Father [will] give good things to those who ask him"* (Mt 7: 8, 11).

Our culture places us in a hotbed of noise, conflicting opinions, and the constant din of information. We are fired on from every side with the demand to listen and pay attention. And, in the end, we are stretched and our ability to concentrate for longer periods of time and think things through is diminished, if not destroyed.

Whereas research shows that noise raises our stress, level and makes us tense, research also demonstrates silence puts us at ease, reduces stress, and promotes general well-being. Herman Melville once wrote, "All profound things...are preceded and attended by silence." When we disengage our brain from external sensory stimuli and place ourselves in silence, we can actually pay attention to our own thoughts and ideas, our feelings and emotions. With such quiet reflection, we can go beyond the surface of the events of our lives, discover meaning, and experience peace.

In the desert, Moses, fleeing in exile for having murdered an Egyptian, came upon the burning bush. Only when he stopped and stood in wonder before it did God speak to him. It was in that reflective silence, he encountered God (see Ex 3:3).

The prophet Elijah, fleeing from King Ahab and his wife Jezebel, came to the same mountain where Moses had encountered God. He took shelter in a cave. There was a strong and violent wind splitting the mountain into pieces, but God was not in the wind. There was a thunderous earthquake, but God was not in the earthquake. Rather, in the gentle, soft barely audible whisper, God was present. In the sound of silence, when Elijah's soul was calm and his mind attentive, he heard God reveal to him what God wanted him to do (see 1 Kgs 19:11-12).

Jesus made silence a priority in His life. After the Father anointed Jesus with the Holy Spirit in His baptism, Jesus did not rush to begin His public ministry. Rather, He went into the solitude of the Judean desert to pray (see Mk 1:12). Throughout His short public ministry, He would not be hurried into action. Prior to every major decision, Jesus set aside time to be silent in prayer before the Father.

Before choosing the twelve apostles, He spent the entire night in prayer on the side of a mountain (see Lk 6:12). After the multiplication of the loaves and fish, when the crowds clamored to crown Christ king, he went up on a mountain to pray by Himself (see Mt 14:23; Jn 6:15). In the last hours of his life, after the Last Supper, He went to the Garden of Gethsemane to pray alone in silence (see Mk 14:32).

Jesus has set the example for all of us. If He, in His humanity untainted by sin, needed moments of silence to think, reflect and, most importantly, to pray, how much more do we! Silence does not come easily to us. We need to discipline ourselves, learn to place a pause in our busy, noise-filled lives and make meaning of our lives. This is at the heart of what it means to be truly human and the way to be filled with the gifts of the Holy Spirit.

In the words of Herman Melville, *"silence is the invisible laying on of the Divine Pontiff's hands upon the world."* Silence releases us from the tyranny of noise. It is not a negative. It is a positive. It is not emptiness and nothingness. It is openness and receptivity before God. As Christopher Jamison so beautifully says, *"Silence is a gateway to the soul, and the soul is the gateway to God."*

Moses spoke of God, but it is the Torah that he gave that leads to the knowledge and love of God. Buddha spoke of Enlightenment, but it is his Noble Path that guides the disciple to achieve it. Mohammed taught about complete submission to Allah, but it is the Koran that instructs the adherent to reach it. In each case, the teacher and the teaching are distinct. But, not with Jesus.

Jesus does more than teach us about the truth. As He told Thomas at the Last

Supper, He tells us, *"I am the way and the truth and the life"* (Jn 14:6). Jesus does not simply point out the way to God. No! He says, *"I am the way."* He alone can say, *"No one comes to the Father except through me"* (Jn 14:6). And the reason is this: Jesus is the very Wisdom of God Incarnate. By using these gifts, we become more and more one with *"Christ Jesus, who became for us wisdom from God, as well as righteousness, sanctification, and redemption"* (1 Cor 1:30).

It is our union with Christ that brings us peace and true happiness not just in this life, but in the life to come. This is the ultimate purpose of all the gifts of the Holy Spirit. *"Through the fear of the Lord, we rise to piety, from piety then to knowledge, from knowledge we derive strength, from strength counsel, with counsel we move towards understanding, and with intelligence towards wisdom and thus, by the sevenfold grace of the Spirit, there opens to us at the end of the ascent the entrance to the life of Heaven"* (Pope St. Gregory the Great, *Homiliae in Hiezechihelem Prophetam*, II 7,7). By joyfully receiving and zealously using the gifts of the Holy Spirit, we find our way to lasting happiness.

Q & A on the Holy Spirit

1. **Who is the Holy Spirit?**

He is the Third Person of the Blessed Trinity, proceeding from Father and Son with Whom He is equal. He is the Love of God personified.

2. **Who particularly revealed the Holy Spirit?**

Jesus Christ Who promised, "When the Spirit of Truth comes, He will guide you into all the truth" (Jn 16:13).

3. **Mention some of the names given to the Holy Spirit.**

Christ called Him Paraclete, translated as Advocate, as "Coach" by Fr. Hopkins the poet, because He exhorts, comforts. The liturgy calls Him Father of the poor, Giver of gifts, Light of hearts. . . .

4. **Where and when was He particularly manifested?**

At Christ's Baptism, and at Pentecost.

5. **Is Pentecost the Feast of the Holy Spirit?**

No, just as there is no Feast of the Father, nor of the Eternal Son, so there is no Feast of the Holy Spirit. Pentecost is the Feast that recalls the marvelous reception of the Holy Spirit by the Infant Church.

6. What then does the Holy Spirit do for the Church?

a. He remains with the Church to sanctify her.

b. He dwells in the Church and in the hearts of the faithful as in a temple.

c. He prays in the faithful making them realize they are indeed beloved adopted children of God.

d. He guides the Church in the way of all truth; hence the frequent invocation of the Holy Spirit, and Masses of the Holy Spirit at Church Councils.

e. He imparts charismatic gifts.

f. He constantly works for the spiritual renewal of the Church, leading her to perfect union with her Spouse. "The Spirit and the Bride [the Church] say, 'Come' " (Rev 22:17).

g. He is the "heart of the Missionary Church." Recall the missionary spirit of the Church after the first Pentecost novena of prayer "with one mind and one heart."

h. Recall His relationship with Mary, Mother of the Church, and with Christ the Head of the Church.

7. But is God's activity in His creation not common to the three Divine Persons?

Yes. But Scripture attributes certain activities particularly to the Holy Spirit (by appropriation) because of the Holy Spirit's particular role in the Trinity. And so St. Paul tells us: "The charity of God has been poured out into our souls by the Holy Spirit Who is given to us" (Rom 5:5). As Fr. Leen said: He is the Love (or Charity) of God personified.

8. **What are some of the things attributed to the Holy Spirit with respect to individual Christians?**

a. We were born again of water and the Holy Spirit.

b. We received a sort of personal Pentecost in Confirmation: "Almighty God, Father of our Lord Jesus Christ, who brought these your servants to new birth by water and the Holy Spirit, freeing them from sin: send upon them, O Lord, the Holy Spirit, the Paraclete" (in Rite of Confirmation).

c. He helps us to make a good confession (know, detest our sins, renounce them out of love of God above all and resolve to change our lives). Recall the Easter gift: "Receive the Holy Spirit. If you forgive the sins of anyone, they are forgiven . . . " (Jn 20:23).

d. He will make us appreciate the Word of God (Holy Scripture) inspired by Him, and it is in that "Spirit" that we must read it.

e. He will likewise make us appreciate the unique value of the Holy Sacrifice of the Mass and the reception of Christ in Holy Communion.

f. He enlightens our minds, strengthens our wills, guides us in making important decisions regarding vocation, overcoming habitual faults, living a life of faith and hope and charity, charity toward God and our neighbor.

9. What then is the value of true Devotion to the Holy Spirit?

When Cardinal Mercier was asked during a Retreat in Brussels what was the "secret of sanctity" he answered: "Every day for five minutes enter into yourself, casting out all distracting thoughts, and in the temple of the Holy Spirit which you are, adore the Holy Spirit. Ask Him to enlighten you, guide, strengthen and console you. Promise Him to submit to that guidance, and with His help to accept all that He permits to happen to you. Ask Him only: 'Make Your will known to me.'"

This is the secret not only of sanctity, but of happiness which the world cannot give.

10. When should I invoke the Holy Spirit?

From what has been said above: You can invoke the Holy Spirit for any spiritual and secular work, for proper reception of the Sacraments, for proper choices, for proper reading of the Scriptures. And to use the words of Fr. Leen, "may you acquire a tender devotion to the Holy Spirit, appreciating His intimate role in Christian life."

Prayers

Prayer to Receive the Holy Spirit

O KING of glory,
    send us the Promised of the Father,
the Spirit of Truth.
May the Counselor Who proceeds from You
enlighten us
and infuse all truth in us,
as You have promised.

Prayer for the Seven Gifts of the Spirit

O LORD Jesus,
    through You I humbly beg the merciful
        Father
to send the Holy Spirit of grace,
that He may bestow upon us His sevenfold gifts.

May He send us the gift of *wisdom,*
which will make us relish the Tree of Life
that is none other than Yourself;
the gift of *understanding,*
which will enlighten us;
the gift of *counsel,*
which will guide us in the way of righteousness;
and the gift of *fortitude,*
which will give us the strength to vanquish
the enemies of our sanctification and salvation.

May He impart to us the gift of *knowledge*,
which will enable us to discern Your teaching
and distinguish good from evil;
the gift of *piety*,
which will make us enjoy true peace;
and the gift of *fear of the Lord*,
which will make us shun all iniquity
and avoid all danger of offending Your Majesty.
To the Father
and to the Son
and to the Holy Spirit
be given all glory and thanksgiving forever.

St. Bonaventure

Prayer for the Twelve Fruits of the Spirit

HOLY Spirit,
eternal Love of the Father and the Son,
kindly bestow on us
the fruit of *charity*,
that we may be united to You by Divine love;
the fruit of *joy*,
that we may be filled with holy consolation;
the fruit of *peace*,
that we may enjoy tranquility of soul;
and the fruit of *patience*,
that we may endure humbly
everything that may be opposed to our own
        desires.

Divine Spirit,
be pleased to infuse in us
the fruit of *benignity,*
that we may willingly relieve our neighbor's
     necessities;
the fruit of *goodness,*
that we may be benevolent toward all;
the fruit of *forbearance,*
that we may not be discouraged by delay
but may persevere in prayer;
and the fruit of *mildness,*
that we may subdue every rising of ill temper,
stifle every murmur,
and repress the susceptibilities of our nature
in all our dealings with our neighbor.

Creator Spirit,
graciously impart to us
the fruit of *fidelity,*
that we may rely with assured confidence
on the word of God;
the fruit of *modesty,*
that we may order our exterior regularly;
and the fruits of *continence* and *chastity,*
that we may keep our bodies in such holiness
as befits Your temple,
so that having by Your assistance
preserved our hearts pure on earth,
we may merit in Jesus Christ,
according to the words of the Gospel,
to see God eternally
in the glory of His Kingdom.